I SEE COLOUR
The Amazing Life of Bolu Davis

Written By:
Barine Ngbor

Illustrated By:
Erica Metta

Monster House Publishing
416 Northumberland St.
Fredericton NB, Canada
E3B 3K4

Copyright text © 2023 Barine Ngbor
Copyright art © 2023 Erica Metta
ISBN 978-1-77785-424-9 (ISBN 978-1-77785-426-3)
First Printing

Design: Danelle Vautour
Editor: Christiana Myers

Monster House Publishing acknowledges the generous support of
the Government of New Brunswick and the Department
of Tourism, Heritage and Culture.

This book is dedicated to my sweet angel sister, Nazor. Keep being the shining star that you are!

TABLE OF CONTENTS

Notes to Our Lovely Parents and Young Readers

In this book, readers have the opportunity to experience and navigate the world through the eyes of Bolu Davis, an eight-year-old Nigerian-Canadian girl. Canada is a multicultural mosaic, and it is important that people recognize the role that culture plays in identity creation while also ensuring that culture is respected and not appropriated. In the title of this book, colour is used to represent the phenotypic differences that exist within the human race, and helps to illustrate that there is not one way to be Black as Black people have a range of skin shades, physical appearances, and cultural backgrounds. Skin conditions such as vitiligo, alopecia, and albinism are also discussed.

 Important core values such as kindness, accountability, friendship, courage, positivity, and the golden rule are emphasized in this book, as well as the message that people should not be treated differently just because they do not look like you. The book also highlights the important role that family plays in who we become. Young children are highly influenced by what they see around them at home and at school, therefore it is the job of parents to create an environment that fosters learning and provides children with the necessary tools to become better people in society.

 "I See Colour" is an educational, fun, and interactive book that presents an opportunity for children and parents to learn and reflect together.

Enjoy!

Bolu Davis

Hello, my name is Bolu Davis, and I am eight years old.

I am a Nigerian-Canadian. Sometimes people ask me which identity I prefer and I never know what to say because I love them both!

My grandma and grandpa live in Nigeria and they give the best hugs. My grandma makes the best Amala and Ewedu in the whole wide world and it is literally my favourite food. Sometimes, during the summer, it gets too hot in Nigeria and I just want to swim in the pool all day.

I was born in Canada, and I love Canada because most of my friends are here. I love making snow angels with them and having snowball fights.

During the winter, my mum usually buys me hot chocolate and Timbits from Tim Hortons. Oh! I love Tim Hortons! There is a similar snack to Timbits in Nigeria, except they are called Puff-Puffs, and I love them too. I love watching cartoons, listening to music with my brother, painting with my dad, and cooking with my mum. I love seeing bright colours because they make me very happy. My favourite colours are taffy and orange. For Christmas, my mum bought me a new pair of orange winter boots and they are so pretty. My room is taffy in colour, which is a shade of pink. Did you know that there are over 100 different shades of pink? Before we meet my friends, let me properly introduce you to my family.

My father's name is
Ayodele Davis and he
is an artist.

My mother's name is
Folake Davis and she
is a scientist.

She gets to do pretty
cool stuff at work,
and I want to be
just like her when I
grow up.

I have an older brother whose name is Timi, and he is ten years old. Although Timi can be very annoying, I love him very much.

He loves listening to music and playing soccer. We also have a golden poodle called Bella, and she gives great cuddles.

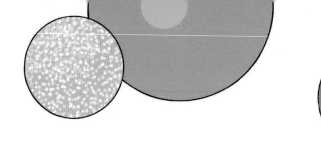

Emillie's Birthday Party

Today is my best friend's birthday and I am excited. I get to eat cake and see most of my friends from school. Emillie and I are like twins except I am just a little bit taller. I sometimes call her my sister because I wish I had one.

Emillie has blue eyes, while I have dark brown eyes. We both have big hair. I have a coily black afro and Emillie has blonde curly hair. We also both have birth marks on the same spot on our faces, and we both love pink. She has a pink room just like mine!

The New Kid at School

It rained at school today so we were not allowed to play outside during recess. Ms. Bumble divided the class into pairs and assigned us a drawing. Jane, the new kid at school, was added to my group. We paired up to work on a butterfly drawing together while Martha and Angelica worked on a school bus drawing across the table. Martha made a few comments about Jane to Angelica that Jane overheard and responded to by saying, "I do not have cancer, I have alopecia."

This caught Ms. Bumble's attention and she decided to address the whole class. By the end of the day, I learned three things. The first was that alopecia is a condition that leads to hair loss. Ms. Bumble mentioned that there were different causes of alopecia, but she did not go into detail. Secondly, she spoke about kindness and the golden rule, which means that you should treat others the way that you would like to be treated. She told Martha that it was wrong to make assumptions about people, and if she really wanted to know something, she could just ask nicely.

Finally, Ms. Bumble spoke about boundaries. She said that just because you ask someone a personal question nicely, it does not guarantee that they will provide an answer. If a person does not feel comfortable answering then they should not be pressured. Martha apologized to Jane, who forgave her, and everybody was happy once again.

Wash Day

I love hair wash days with my dad because it is fun and sometimes we get to bop to music that we both like. Other times, he tells me stories of what it was like growing up as a little boy in Ibadan, Nigeria.

My dad is putting my hair in space buns today and it is one of my favourite styles because it is so cute. I love my hair so much because it is healthy, soft, beautiful, and smells like coconut candy.

The versatility of my hair brings me joy. I can do whatever I want to do with it! Most times I wear it in an afro, sometimes I wear it in braids or puffs, and occasionally I wear it straight.

At night, I wear my orange silk bonnet to protect my curls. My hair is nurtured with love, patience, good protective styling, and with my wash day routine.

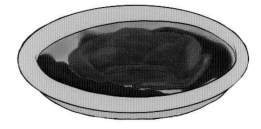

Cultural Day at School

This is the first time that we are celebrating cultural day at school, and I am excited. We get to talk about our culture, wear our cultural attire, and bring our cultural dishes to school. Ms. Bumble said we could do whatever we were comfortable with. Some people spoke about their culture, wore clothes, and brought food, while others chose to only participate in one or two activities. Culture is the way of life of a group of people. People experience and express their cultures through languages, food, music, traditions, and clothing. Ms. Bumble also said that culture should be appreciated and not appropriated because it is disrespectful to appropriate someone else's culture.

Bolu

For school today, I wore my Iro and Buba that my grandma made for me. In Yoruba culture, when greeting our elders, the girls should curtsy while the boys bow. As a Yoruba girl, this is how we greet others throughout the different times of the day.

"E káàro means"
good morning

"E káàsan means"
good afternoon

"E Kú alè means"
good evening

I brought amala and abula, which is a mixture of gbegiri, ewedu, and stew to school. The ewedu soup is made from jute leaves. My mum also adds spices, crayfish, and locust beans. I love locust beans. In some cultures people use cutlery to eat, while in others they use chopsticks. In my culture, we use our hands to eat. I can't wait for you to meet my friends!

Harshita

Hello, my name is Harshita, and I am a Tamil girl from India. My name means "happy person" or "someone who is full of happiness." I am currently wearing my beautiful Pattu Pavadai, which is usually worn on special occasions and for traditional festivals.

My father owns an Indian restaurant downtown, and today he made me dosa, chutneys, and sambar for breakfast. I also brought some panipuri snacks, my absolute favourite.

Emillie

Bonjour! Je m'appelle Emillie. I am bilingual and I speak both French and English. I am from Montréal, Québec.

Today, I brought with me the poutine that my mamie made. Poutine is a French-Canadian dish made with french fries, gravy, and cheese.

Sofia

Hola amigos, my name is Sofia and I am Mexican. Last week my sister celebrated her quinceañera and she looked so beautiful in her dress. I can't wait to celebrate my own quinceañera.

Today, I brought carne asada tacos, which are beef tacos made with soft corn tortillas.

Nehan

Hey, my name is Nehan and I am Nepalis. My country is the only country in the world that does not have a rectangular flag.

Nepal is also the home of one of the tallest mountains in the world, Mount Everest.

Damerae

Hello, my name is Damerae and I am from Jamaica. Did you know that Jamaica is the third largest island in the Caribbean Sea? In Jamaica, our official language is English, but Patois is also very common.

We are globally known for our rich culture, great music, and carnivals. Today, my mother made ackee and saltfish—music to my ears!

Akio

Konnichiwa! Watashi no namae wa Akio and I am Japanese. Today I brought sushi with me that my sobo made. In my culture, we are taught to respect our elders.

In Japan, we have various festivals and holidays. My favourite is Oshogatsu, which is the new year celebration. I get to spend it with my family every year.

Play Date

Twice a week, Emillie and I go swimming. Right now, we are learning how to swim in the deep end. I find it a bit scary, but my mum says starting new things can be scary and sometimes you must leave your comfort zone by pushing yourself. She also said that sometimes she still gets scared as an adult, and it is totally fine as long as you are trying.

After swimming lessons, my mum took us to get ice cream and some Timbits. Emillie got strawberry ice cream, while I got vanilla. I don't think I have stressed enough how much I love Timbits, especially the honey dip ones!

Then we went to the park and I had so much fun.

By the time we got home, I was exhausted.

Kids Can be Mean Too

When we got home after school, my brother Timi did not seem like his usual cheerful, mischievous self. I could tell something was wrong. Apparently, some kids at school made fun of him and called him some terrible names during soccer practice.

Mum was not happy about the situation so she called the school and the principal said the situation was going to be handled.

Mum then made us breakfast for
dinner. We had pancakes with
syrup, whipped cream,
and strawberries.

Timi seemed to be in a better mood, which made me happy.

The next day, Mum had a meeting with the principal and the parents of the other kids. The kids were genuinely sorry but, as punishment, they still had to arrange the class art station for a week instead of attending recess and soccer practice. Since they were sorry and Timi seemed to have moved past it, you might be wondering why they still had consequences. The reason is accountability.

Being accountable means that you take responsibility for your actions whether they are good or bad. For example, the boys apologizing to Timi did not automatically erase their hurtful words. Accountability helps you understand why what you did was wrong by giving you the opportunity to reflect on it and set things right. I, too, have had to take accountability for some of my actions in the past. Mum also mentioned that even though some actions have consequences, people can also be rewarded for good behaviour.

Melanin
(There is no one way to be Black)

My brother Timi has a skin condition called vitiligo and I think that makes him unique. Some pretty cool people also have vitiligo like Winnie Harlow, a Jamaican-Canadian supermodel. Doctors are not 100% sure of the cause of vitiligo, but most believe it is an autoimmune disorder that affects melanocytes, the cells responsible for producing melanin. Melanin is a pigment produced by our bodies that helps protect us from the sun's ultraviolet rays, which can be damaging to the skin. People of African descent and people who live in areas that have more intense sunlight are usually darker than others for this reason. There is not just one way to be Black as your skin tone does not automatically determine your race and ethnicity. Some people have light skin, while some have dark skin, and some have an olive tone.

Christmas, my Favourite Time of the Year

It started snowing today and that means Christmas is around the corner. I am excited because Christmas is my favourite time of the year. We get to make gingerbread houses as a family, open presents from Santa, drink hot chocolate, and watch Christmas movies. This year my cousin Modu and her parents are coming to spend the Christmas holiday with us. I have already started my countdown and I am over the moon. Modu is one of my best friends, and I can't wait to see her.

Modupe

Hello, my name is Modupe, and I am a person with albinism. Albinism is a genetic condition that causes some people to have little to no melanin, which affects their skin, hair, and eye colour.

To protect myself from the sun I wear sunscreen, sunglasses, and use an umbrella.

Christmas Day

On Christmas Day, we woke up to the smell of freshly baked cookies and hot chocolate. It was time to open presents. Mum got Modu and I matching dresses. I was glad Modu loved the gift I got her—a new doll. She got me some Nigerian snacks, chin chin and plantain chips, my absolute favourite.

This year, I am grateful for a lot of things. Most importantly, I am grateful that my family gets to spend another wonderful Christmas together. What are you grateful for?

Barine Ngbor is a Nigerian writer who currently resides in Canada. She has always considered herself a storyteller, and took an interest in writing from the early age of six. She is currently working on her first novel and her second children's book. When she is not writing, she spends her time reading, swimming, painting, or enjoying time with her family. She recently graduated with a Bachelor of Science in biochemistry and psychology and, one day, hopes to become a plastic surgeon in order to work with children who have cleft lips.

Erica Metta is a self-taught artist and illustrator from Nigeria who works with digital media. Her art features expressive characters and bold colours that come together to tell stories. She has created illustrations for a variety of projects that include album covers, brand designs, and children's books. She is currently based in the United States where she is completing a masters degree in electrical engineering.